FAITH TO STAY CALM IN A CRISIS

I0169600

Unless otherwise noted, all scriptural citations are

taken from the Authorized (King James and

Amplified) Version of the Bible.

ISBN: 978-0-9963430-3-9

log on to: www.kwa.life

KESZA Publishing LLC

P.O. Box 1295

Marrero, LA 70073

ACKNOWLEDGMENTS

I give honor and thanks to God for His Holy Spirit who is within me, teaching me, and guiding me through awesome projects like this and others. He is my source of inspiration.

Thanks to my lovely wife, Ethel, for your continuous support and dedication throughout the years. We have been life mates and partners for over twenty years now. I look forward to the next twenty years.

Thanks to my children, Seth & the late Zachary. You have been the joy of my life, and teaching you, and watching you grow, has been exciting. God has wonderful love for you and plans for you.

FAITH TO STAY CALM IN A CRISIS

Much love to my wonderful and faithful congregation of Royal Palace Ministries & the partners of KWA Ministries International. We have been through much together and conquered all. I love you all, and you are by far the best group of people in this world!

Faith To Stay Calm In A Crisis

Seven Ways To Stay Calm In A Crisis

FAITH TO STAY CALM IN A CRISIS

Table Of Contents   Pages

Introduction

There are times in your life when things just don't seem right. You find yourself faced with all sorts of obstacles. There are things that happen in your life that are out of your control. What do you do when things go wrong? What do you do when you're faced with obstacles that you did not cause? How do you handle problems that arise? Where do you go when you don't know what to do? It is my prayer that this book will be a source of information that can help you navigate through life's ups and downs. It is the purpose of this book to provide you with information that can help you to stay calm in a crisis. As you read from chapter to chapter, I will provide you with information that can help you navigate issues that arise in your life that seem out of your control. I believe that no matter what life throws at you, there is a way that you can stay calm as you figure out how to handle it. Let's take a journey through the pages of this book and discover how. Just because you may be surprised by life, you don't have to be in a panic or filled with anxiety and worry. You can face life's issues, both good and bad, and at the same time stay calm.

Chapter One

Christ Calculated

The Crisis

FAITH TO STAY CALM IN A CRISIS

A crisis is a condition of instability or danger, as in social, economic, political, or international affairs, leading to a decisive change. It is a dramatic or circumstantial upheaval in a person's life. It is during these times of crisis that we often wonder how we're going to make it. Sometimes in life things just happen. Things sometimes seem out of our control. The question is when these crises arise, how do you handle them? What do you do when your life seems like it's turned upside down to no fault of your own and it was nothing that you did? Let's take a look at God's Inaugural Purpose to see if it was His original intent for you to be going through crisis.

His Inaugural Purpose

The good news is that before you got here, before you were even born, before you were a thought in your parents' mind or a glimmer in their eyes, God had a plan that would include calculating every crisis that would happen in your life. That plan included sending His only begotten son Jesus Christ into this world to carry your burdens and to carry your sins to the cross and die. The Bible says in the book of Isaiah 53: 4-12, Surely He has borne our griefs (sicknesses, weaknesses, and distresses) and carried our sorrows and pains [*of punishment*], yet we [*ignorantly*] considered Him stricken, smitten, and afflicted by God [*as if with leprosy*]. But He was wounded for our transgressions, He was bruised for our guilt and iniquities; the chastisement [*needful to obtain*] peace and well-being for us was upon Him, and with the stripes [*that wounded*] Him we are healed and made whole. All we like sheep have gone astray, we have turned everyone to his own way; and the Lord has made to light upon Him the guilt and iniquity of us all. He was oppressed, [*yet when*] He was afflicted, He was submissive and opened not His mouth; like a lamb that is led to the slaughter, and as a sheep before her shearers is dumb, so He opened not His mouth. By oppression and judgment He was taken away; and as for His generation, who among them considered that He was cut off out of the land of the living [*stricken to His death*] for the transgression of my [*Isaiah's*]

people, to whom the stroke was due? And they
assigned Him a grave with the wicked, and with a
rich man in His death, although He had done no
violence, neither was any deceit in His mouth. Yet
it was the will of the Lord to bruise Him; He has
put Him to grief and made Him sick. When You
and He make His life an offering for sin [*and He
has risen from the dead, in time to come*], He shall
see His [*spiritual*] offspring, He shall prolong His
days, and the will and pleasure of the Lord shall
prosper in His hand. He shall see [*the fruit*] of the
travail of His soul and be satisfied; by His
knowledge of Himself [*which He possesses and
imparts to others*] shall My [*uncompromisingly*]
righteous One, My Servant, justify many and make
many righteous (upright and in right standing with

God), for He shall bear their iniquities and their guilt [*with the consequences, says the Lord*]. Therefore will I divide Him a portion with the great [*kings and rulers*], and He shall divide the spoil with the mighty, because He poured out His life unto death, and [*He let Himself*] be regarded as a criminal and be numbered with the transgressors; yet He bore [*and took away*] the sin of many and made intercession for the transgressors (the rebellious).

As you can clearly see, it lays out for us God's predestined plan for our salvation; and, not just for our salvation, but to give us a life full of abundance. Jesus died so we could live free of fear, worry, anxiety, and the stress of this world. He gave it all for your success and healing. It was

His plan from the beginning to make sure that you would be healed and safe from hurt and danger. Jesus gave His life so that you can get yours. Let's now look at His plan to assure if things go wrong in this life, you would have a way to protect yourself, and that protection is provided by His sacrifice.

His Immunization Plan

Again, the Bible says in Revelation 13: 8, And all the inhabitants of the earth will fall down in adoration and pay him homage, everyone whose name has not been recorded in the Book of Life of the Lamb that was slain [*in sacrifice*] from the foundation of the world. We are repeatedly told by God that He has made a way for us long before we were born.

FAITH TO STAY CALM IN A CRISIS

At the time of this book, the world is dealing with COVID 19. COVID 19 is a respiratory sickness that is causing the world to be in a crisis. The president and his staff have issued a stay-at-home order. They are asking that we stay at home except to go out and purchase groceries or to go to the pharmacy. Schools are closed, and they have been closed for several weeks now. The unemployment rate is at an all-time high. People are dying at an alarming rate, and hospitals are saying that they don't have enough ventilators to deal with this crisis. We are now being told that if we leave our homes we should wear gloves and a face mask. The world is rocking because of this virus. There is panic and fear running rampant through the land, and it is understandable that people are concerned about their lives and the lives of their love ones. We are uncertain if the world will ever return back to a state of normalcy. I believe that forever there will be a new normal, but even in the midst of all of the uncertainties, I believe that there is an answer. That answer is understanding that before this pandemic hit this world, God had calculated the crisis that He already knew we would be facing. That's why the Bible says in the book of Revelation 13: 8 that Jesus was slain from the foundation of the world. You see beloved, Jesus is the answer to all of your problems. He knew that you would be faced with this invisible enemy called the coronavirus, and so He went to the cross and died nailing every sickness and disease to the cross. If you were to simply believe in Him and

His finished work on the cross, He promises that He is here for you, and you don't have to live in fear of this disease. You don't have to live in fear, but in faith. I know it's difficult to believe because you're asking yourself if God loves the world so much, then why is He allowing or causing such calamities to hit this world? How can He sit idly by and do nothing while innocent people are dying on a daily basis? The world is experiencing over 1,000 people dying from the coronavirus a day. Where is God? Why isn't He doing something? If He is love, then where is He?

Understanding the Love of God

I know that it is very difficult for you to understand how God can allow such calamities and not get involved, but I want to explain to you how this works. In the beginning God created a world, and then He created Adam and Eve. He placed in their hands the authority and the dominion to reign and to subdue this world. You see beloved, God created the world, but He gave the world to humans. He is always ready to help and assist you in your everyday life, but He has given the authority to govern this world to us, and so I submit to you that God is not the cause of this coronavirus. He is not idly sitting by and not doing anything. He loves us unconditionally, but just like when He sent Jesus here, He had to ask

Mary for permission to use Her body, because He could not just put Jesus on the earth without going through the proper channels. So it is in your daily life, He won't just break in and take over. You must invite Him into your situations, and you must ask Him to assist you and to help you navigate through life situations. I promise you He stands ready to get involved and to help in every area of your life.

Listen to what the Bible says in the book of Psalms 115: 16: the Heavens are the Lord's heavens, but the earth has He given to the children of men.

It is vital that you understand that God is not an Indian giver; He will never give you something and then take it away from you or try to control what you do. He loves you endlessly, but He will not illegally invade your life. He will long to get involved, but He needs your permission. God desires to partner in this life with you. He wants to help. He wants to heal. He wants to bring peace and calm, and to take away the anxiety, but He is waiting for you to ask Him for help and to do the necessary things that are needed to partner with Him as He helps.

His Impervious Proclamation

Impervious means incapable of being penetrated or affected, and proclamation is an official public declaration or announcement. That's why it's important for you to proclaim that you're healed and not sick. It's important for you to say it for yourself; no one can do this for you. Remember, the power to heal is not your responsibility. It's

God who does the

healing; you simply must believe and speak to

receive it. There are various categories of faith,

and reigning faith is that which lays hold to what

God has promised and refuses to let go!

I want you to say, I've been delivered, and I'm not

going back! This is why confession is so

important.

There are three ways confession is released:

- Confession is released in my prayer- I JN. 5:14.
- Confession is released in my proclamation.
- Confession is released in my praise-
  ISA. 57:19, HEB. 13:15.

FAITH TO STAY CALM IN A CRISIS

There are multiple ways healing was ministered to

individuals with manifestations that are both

immediate and progressive. Let's look at seven of

those ways. I will list them with the scripture to

show where you can find them in the Bible.

Seven ways healing is ministered in the New

Testament Church:

1. Prayer cloth- **ACTS 19:11-12**
2. Exercise of faith- **MK: 9:29**
3. Laying on of hands- **MK: 16:18**
4. Anointing with oil- **JS: 5:13-14**
5. The prayer of agreement- **MTT: 18:19**
6. Prayer of faith- **JS: 5:14, MK: 11:24**
7. Gift of healing- **JN: 11:1-4**

I want you to read this health confession out loud

and allow the words to resonate in you. Let it be

your new mantra.

HEALTH CONFESSION

Father, I thank you that by the stripes of Jesus I am healed, resisting sickness and disease. I boldly declare that I walk in divine health in my body, my mind, and my emotions in the name of Jesus. I thank you, Father, that because of my covenant and because I honor and worship you, no plague or epidemic comes near or into my house, affecting me or my family. Every harmful germ, virus, or disease that touches my body must die immediately. God, I thank you that you satisfy my lips with those foods that are good and healthy for my body. I will live and not die so I may continue to declare the works of the Lord in the name of Jesus. Amen!

FAITH TO STAY CALM IN A CRISIS

Please list your prayer needs and testimonies

here:

_____

_____

_____

_____

_____

_____

_____

_____

_____

_____

Chapter Two

Cognitive Confidence
In Calvary

> **Until you make the unconscious conscious, it will direct your life and you will call it fate!!!!! - Carl Jung-**

I think that it is imperative that you begin to understand that you must have a cognitive confidence in the cross of Jesus Christ. What does it mean to be cognitive? Cognitive is the active process of knowing, perception, product of such a process relating to the mental process of knowing, receiving memory, judgment, and reasoning. In a nut shell, to be cognitive is to have a process by which you use your thinking to process information. As it relates to staying calm in a crisis, the question is, how do you stay calm when crisis arises in your life? The way that you process the information is extremely imperative because it will alert all of your emotions to either everything is all right, or it will alert your emotions to begin to panic and to live in fear.

Developing A Thought Process

What you must do now is to develop a process by which you can stay calm in every crisis that life may throw at you.

The Bible says in Isaiah 53: 1-5, who has believed (trusted in relied upon and clung to) our message (of that which was revealed to us)? And to whom has the arm of the Lord been disclosed? For (the servant of God) grew up before Him like a tender plant, and like a route out of dry ground; He has no form or comeliness (royal, kingly pomp), that we should look at Him, and no beauty that we should

desire Him. He was despised and rejected and

forsaken by men, a Man of sorrows and pains and

acquainted with grief and sickness; and like one

from whom men hid their faces, He was despised,

and we did not appreciate His work or have any

esteem for Him. Surely he has borne our grief's

(sicknesses, weaknesses, and distresses) and

carried our sorrows and pains (of punishment), yet

we (ignorantly) considered him stricken, smitten,

and afflicted by God (as if with leprosy). But He

was wounded for our transgressions, He was

bruised for our guilt and iniquities; the

chastisement (needed to obtain) peace and well-

being for us was upon Him, and with the stripes

(that wounded) Him, we are healed and made

whole. As you can see, the Bible explicitly explains what Jesus Christ did for you on the cross, before you was born, and before you became a glimmer in your parents eyes. Jesus died on the cross, so when I say you must be cognitive confident in Calvary, you must put your trust in the finished work of Jesus Christ. He had a plan for you long before you needed an answer. God provided an answer in the form of His only son Jesus Christ. He came, He lived, and He died, and when you are cognitive conscious of the information that He died for your sins, then your confidence in his finished work will allow you to stay calm in any crisis life may throw at you.

> Remember that Carl Jung says, until you make the unconscious conscious, it will direct your life, and you will call it fate.

Now, fate is an outcome determined by certain actions. The key here is to make your unconscious mind become your conscious mind, because 95% of your awakened state is governed by your subconscious mind and 5% is governed by your conscious mind (Szegedy-Maszak 2005).

According to Dr. Bruce H. Lipton, the greatest problem we face is that we think we are running our lives with the wishes, desires, and aspirations created by our conscious mind. When we struggle or fail to obtain our goals, we are generally led to conclude that we are victims of outside forces preventing us from reaching our destination.

That means we run our lives while we are awake and conscious by our subconscious mind. 95% of what we think and how we act and decisions we make are governed by our subconscious mind.

You may ask, why is this important? It is important because what you allow to enter your mind eventually makes its way to your subconscious mind, which will end up being like a law to you. It will shape your will. You will eventually make all of your decisions through the lens of information you have allowed to enter your mind; be it subliminally or consciously. That information walked past your will and entered your subconscious mind where, as I'd like to put it, sits on the shelves of your subconscious mind waiting to be used while you are consciously deciding or thinking about what to do.

This is extremely important. Again, let me repeat. 95% of your decision making is housed in your subconscious mind. Only 5% of your decision-making is in your conscious mind.

Having said that, let's look at the belief system to determine how you can make the necessary changes to how you have been thinking concerning crisis.

The Belief System- What is It?

What is your belief system? What does it mean to say belief system? A belief system is a set of ideas, thoughts, and opinions. Where did they come from? They came from the time you were born. You learn various things in life. Your belief system was being shaped by the way you see life. It is the way that you navigate through life. It is how you make decisions. It is how you perceive things to be. A belief system is extremely important.

Let me show you a story in the Bible to help explain how important your belief system is.

In the book of Mark 9:18, there was a man who had a son, and his son was vexed with an evil spirit. The evil spirit often threw the young man in the fire. It threw him down to the ground, causing him to convulse. The man brought his son to Jesus's disciples in order for them to heal him, but Jesus's disciples were unable to cast the demons out of the young man. The father then decided to bring his son to Jesus.

Jesus replied in verse 19, and He answered them all, O unbelieving generation, without any faith, how long shall I have to do with you, how long am I to bear with you, bring him to me.

Look at Jesus's response to the father's son in verse 20. It says they brought the boy to Him, and when the spirit saw Him, at once it completely convulsed the boy. He fell to the ground and kept rolling about foaming at the mouth, and Jesus said to his father, how long has he had this? He answered, from the time he was a little boy, and it has often thrown him over into the fire, intending to kill him. But, if you can do anything, do have pity on us and help us.

I want you to pay close attention to what Jesus's response was. Listen to what Jesus says in verse 23. Jesus said you say to me, if you can do anything, why, all things can be possible to him who believes. The father of the boy gave an eager piercing and articulate cry with tears, and he said, "Lord, I believe constantly." Help my weakness of faith, another translation says, help my unbelief.

FAITH TO STAY CALM IN A CRISIS

To believe or to have belief simply means to be confident and to have faith or trust in the possibilities. It is to simply believe that Jesus has the power to do what you're asking Him to do, and when I say the belief system, what is it again? It is all of the information that you have accumulated down through the years that has shaped the way you think and the way you believe. This is so crucial because whenever you are about to make a decision, whenever you are about to decide one way or the other, it is your belief system that says how do you see it, what do you think about it, and how did you handle it in the past?

Since we realized that our belief system sets the way that we react to crisis, emergencies, and situations, it is imperative that you make some changes to your belief system. For example, maybe the way that you handle crisis is to become paranoid. What is paranoid and what does it mean to be paranoid? Paranoid is a mental insanity marked by systematic delusion. That is when crisis arises in your life. Your belief system and your subconscious mind tells your conscious mind to panic and to handle the situation in a state of frenzy; so, it is important that you reset your belief system and move from a paranoia state.

This can be accomplished by my second point, and that is the biology of belief. Understanding how the belief system works - not just understanding what it is, but understanding how it works with us on a daily basis to accomplish what we believe and how we handle what we believe. Let's look at the biology of belief.

The Biology of Belief- How It Works

The meaning of Soul is (psyche) the mind in a human, or other conscious being, the element, part, substance, or process that reasons, thinks, feels, wills, perceives, and judges.

The conscious mind, which represents the seat of our personal identity, source, or spirit—is the creative mind. It can see into the future, review the past, or disconnect from the present moment as it solves problems in our head. In its creative capacity, the "conscious mind holds our wishes, desires, and aspirations for our lives. It is the mind that conjures up our positive thoughts."

The Subconscious- existing or operating in the mind beneath or beyond consciousness: record-playback mechanism, habitual, instincts, experiences, acquires behavior belief. The subconscious mind is primarily a repository of stimulus-response tapes derived from instincts and learned experiences. The subconscious mind is fundamentally habitual; it will play the same behavioral responses to life's signals over and over again, much to our chagrin. How many times have you found yourself going ballistic over something trivial like an open cereal box? You have been trained since childhood to carefully close it, but when it's left open, it can drive you bonkers.

The biology of belief is the way that your mind helps you think, to ration, to make decisions, and to navigate through life. You can see that it is important. Not only do you understand how your belief system works, but also how you will believe.

Let me give you an example of how all of this works.

Your mind has two components:

1.) Conscious Mind- when you are awake and you're in an awaken state.

2.) Subconscious Mind- that is your belief system filled with information from the duration of your life. All of your life you have been storing information in your subconscious mind.

I like to call it the warehouse of your mind. This is the place where everything you allowed to enter is stored. Picture it this way: picture an 18-wheeler truck pulling up to a warehouse and unloading groceries off of the truck into the warehouse. The workers would unpack the truck and load the warehouse, so it is with your mindset, your subconscious mind has been storing information that you have allowed to enter your mind. Let me explain. You have what is called will power. You have been given a free will. You can choose to live your life the way you want as long as you don't break any laws. You can live where you want, eat what you want, go where you want, wake up when you want, put on whatever clothes you want, wear whatever style of hair you desire, and you have a free will to make those choices. Your will, which is your decisions, your likes, your wants, your choices is set by you.

Now picture this - how does information enter your subconscious? Whatever you read through your eye gate, whatever you hear through your ear gate, goes through the door of your conscious mind into the warehouse of your subconscious mind; and, it's stored there for future use.

There is a saying that I started the chapter with and that is, until you make your subconscious your conscious, it will direct your life, and you will call it fate. You will begin to believe that you're not in control of your own life but that things will automatically happen without your control. Your mind has been filled with information that passed your will and was given permission by you to be in your subconscious.

Thoughts will be what govern your life. Remember, 95% of your awaken state is governed by your subconscious thoughts. That means while you are awake and trying to make decisions, those decisions are pulled from the warehouse of your subconscious mind. Have you ever asked yourself why do I continually do the same things over and over again? Yes, because it is how you shaped your subconscious mind to make decisions.

If you want a change in the things you've been

doing, you must change the way you think.

Listen to what the scriptures say about changing

your mind.

I beseech you therefore, brethren, by the mercies
of God, that ye present your bodies a living
sacrifice, holy, acceptable unto God, *which is* your
reasonable service. And be not conformed to this
world: but be ye transformed by the renewing of
your mind, that ye may prove what *is* that good,
and acceptable, and perfect, will of God.

Romans 12:1-2 (King James Bible)

Let me give you an example of how you can

change or transform your mind. Remember this -

the subconscious mind shapes opinions. For

example, it is a fact that you may have lost $200,

but it is your opinion if you are ruined or disgraced

[44]

because of the $200 loss. Your subconscious mind shapes your opinion and thoughts that you have allowed to be in your subconscious mind. It will shape your opinion about the loss of $200. Our subconscious stores information through our senses, rather it's truth or lies. We based our actions upon all of the things we have seen and heard and trusted. Our decisions are based on subconscious thoughts that subliminally entered in. So if we are going to be effectively changing the way we think, we are first going to have to clean up the way we think. We need to wash out one to make room for the new and replace a faulty way of thinking with a new, more firm solid way of thinking.

Thought Transformation

Let me give an example of how you can do that. First, get to know the truth and only allow factual, true information into your thoughts. Second, saturate your mind with truth because truth matters. It is only the truth that has the promise to set you free. Third, decide to meditate on truth, to be continuously contemplating over and over until you become one with the way you think. Fourth, show a proof by reasoning and evidence that truth can be demonstrated. Fifth, declare positively and be willing to stand by what you now know to be true. Sixth, transformation of the mind has happened, and that's when the change come. You've changed or altered completely in your nature and in your function. You had a metamorphosis. Let me repeat: Information, Saturation, Meditation, Demonstration, Affirmation, and Transformation.

The Blessings Of Biblical Belief- The Benefits

Now this leads me to the third point of belief and that is the blessing of Biblical belief. You must begin to embrace that the Bible is true. The Bible says in the book of St. John 8: 32 that you will know the truth, and the truth will set you free. Do you see there is a blessing in Biblical belief, and that blessing is freedom? You must embrace and come to grips with your belief in the Bible. Let the Bible be your guidance. Let the word of God, which is given from God, be your final word.

This is important because your belief system is set by the criterias you set, so you determine what you believe, and you determine what you believe to be true. So let me close this chapter by giving you some words from God's Bible that can help shape your thoughts as it relates to staying calm in a crisis. The Bible says in Proverbs 12: 21 that no (actual) evil, misfortune, or calamity shall come upon the righteous, but the wicked shall be filled with evil, misfortune, and calamity.

Decide to make that true in your life. God said He will not allow evil or calamity to come upon you.

By replacing old thoughts with new thoughts, by replacing worldly thoughts with Biblical truth, you have re-established your thoughts not on the shakiness and uncertainties of the world, but with the firm foundation of God's word.

HEALTH CONFESSION

Father, I thank you that by the stripes of Jesus I am healed, resisting sickness and disease. I boldly declare that I walk in divine health in my body, my mind, and my emotions in the name of Jesus. I thank you, Father, that because of my covenant and because I honor and worship you, no plague or epidemic comes near or into my house, affecting me or my family. Every harmful germ, virus, or disease that touches my body must die immediately. God, I thank you that you satisfy my lips with those foods that are good and healthy for my body. I will live and not die so may continue to declare the works of the Lord, in the name of

Jesus. Amen!

Please list your prayer needs and testimonies here:

_____

_____

_____

_____

_____

_____

_____

_____

_____

_____

Chapter Three

**Comfort In
Christ Covering**

FAITH TO STAY CALM IN A CRISIS

At that time Jesus began to say, I thank You, Father, Lord of heaven and earth [*and I acknowledge openly and joyfully to Your honor*], that You have hidden these things from the wise and clever and learned, and revealed them to babies [*to the childish, untaught, and unskilled*]. Yes, Father, [*I praise You that*] such was Your gracious will and good pleasure. All things have been entrusted and delivered to Me by My Father; and no one fully knows and accurately understands the Son except the Father, and no one fully knows and accurately understands the Father except the Son and anyone to whom the Son deliberately wills to make Him known. Come to Me, all you who labor and are heavy-laden and overburdened, and I will cause you to rest. [*I will ease and relieve and refresh your souls.*] Take My yoke upon you and learn of Me, for I am gentle (meek) and humble (lowly) in heart, and you will find rest (relief and ease and refreshment and recreation and blessed quiet) for your souls.For My yoke is wholesome (useful, good--not harsh, hard, sharp, or pressing, but comfortable, gracious, and pleasant), and My burden is light and easy to be borne.

Matthew 11:30 (Amplified Bible)

There's undoubtedly comfort found in the covering of Christ. I love what it says in Matthew 11: 28-30, He says come to me all you who are labored and heavy laden and overburdened.

Listen to what He says in those scriptures. If you are labored and heavy laden and overburdened in a time where COVID 19 is spreading as rapidly as wildfires, people are panicking and living in fear. You are wondering if the job is going to re-open and wondering what life is going to be like. Jesus says if you are heavy laden and if you are labored and overburdened that you can come to Him, and He will cover you. He will cause you to find rest. Now, I hear what you're saying in your mind. You are asking the question, "are you telling me that in the midst of one of the world's worst pandemics in history, Christ can cause me to rest?" My friend, that's exactly what I'm telling you. Christ promises to cover you not just from the pandemic, but in the midst of the pandemic. You see, this rest is a mental rest. This mental rest is more important than bodily rest because you could lay down in a bed, you can actually go to sleep and try to rest your body, but if your mind is racing and unsettled, ultimately there will be no rest - not until you learn to settle your mind, will your body rest. So you see what He's promising is more than physical rest; He is promising that if you would come to Him not just in good times but also in troubled times, that there is a rest provided by Him that you won't find anywhere else.

Let's take a look at condemnation, and see how it can affect the way you see yourself, and ultimately the way you see God.

Condemnation

Condemnation is the devil's weapon to keep you from having confidence in God. If he can get you to keep doubting God and yourself, he will cause you to walk in fear, anxiety, and worry. It is this condemnation that creates a wall between you and God. That's why Jesus says to come to Him to find real answers for life's problems. Listen to what the Bible says in the book of I John.

Whenever our hearts in [*tormenting*] self-accusation make us **feel guilty and condemn us**. [*For we are in God's hands.*] For He is above and greater than our consciences (our hearts), and He knows (perceives and understands) everything [*nothing is hidden from Him*]. And, beloved, if our consciences (our hearts) do not accuse us [*if they do not make us feel guilty and condemn us*], **we have confidence (complete assurance and boldness) before God,** And we receive from Him whatever we ask, because we [*watchfully*] obey His orders [*observe His suggestions and injunctions, follow His plan for us*] and [*habitually*] practice what is pleasing to Him.

I John 3:20-22 (Amplified Bible)

Notice how important it is for you not to let self-condemnation enter your heart. It will create a wall between you and God's truth. This is why Jesus's desire is for you to come to Him to find real rest. This is why I covered in the last chapter the importance of your belief system. The way you think will govern your life decisions. It will help you or hurt you.

Conscious Decision to Come to Christ

Listen to the three categories of problems Jesus listed in Matthew 11:

1.) Labor- to feel fatigue, to work hard, toil, be wearied.

2.)Laden- to load up like animal, to overburden with ceremonies, are spiritual anxiety, burden.

3.) Burden- something carried, of task imposed by the scribes, Pharisees and lawyers, weighed down religion. He made a promise to relieve you of all of these problems if you come to Him.

The three promises of comfort He made were to:

FAITH TO STAY CALM IN A CRISIS

1.) Ease- to cause or permit one to cease from any labor or movement, so as to recover strength. It implies previous toil and care. Its chief significance is that of taking, or causing to take, rest.

2.) Relieve- to be strong enough for, to ward off, or to aid.

3.) Refresh- to give intermission from labor, to give rest, to cause to cease our **Souls**- (the seat of sentiment element in man, that by which he perceives, reflects, feels, desires, will).

He wants to bring understanding concerning life issues so you can rest in Him. There's a real refreshing that come with Jesus. He is the only one who can remove every problem you're faced with.

He is the only one who is true to His word. In a world where you are lied to on a continual basis; Jesus promises to be honest and true with you. His promises are priceless.

Life can sometimes find you toiling for the things that you think are important, only to leave you thirsting for more. Life cannot and will not remove burdens from you. It will only pile them on you more.

Listen to a story of a man in the Bible who was dealing with some real issues. He decided to bring his issues to God. Let's read about what happened.

Three times I called upon the Lord and besought [*Him*] about this and begged that it might depart from me; But He said to me, My grace (My favor and loving-kindness and mercy) is enough for you

FAITH TO STAY CALM IN A CRISIS

[sufficient against any danger and enables you to bear the trouble manfully]; for My strength and power are made perfect (fulfilled and completed) and show themselves most effective in *[your]* weakness. Therefore, I will all the more gladly glory in my weaknesses and infirmities, that the strength and power of Christ (the Messiah) may rest (yes, may pitch a tent over and dwell) upon me!

II Corinthians 12:8 (Amplified Bible)

Notice in the story that the Apostle Paul was

dealing with a thorn in his flesh, which was an evil

spirit tempting him every time he tried to

accomplish something. Every time he tried to do

something, this evil spirit would hinder him and

stand in the way. Paul became so frustrated and so

aggravated with this that he decided to take it to

God, so he prayed and asked God to remove this

infirmity from him. Pay close attention to the response. God said, My grace, My safe and loving kindness and mercy is enough for you against any danger and enables you to bear the trouble. He literally just told Paul that His grace, which is unmerited, unearned, and undeserved favor was enough to manage the problem because when Paul was weak, God strength was made perfect in him. I'm telling you that by the grace of God, you too can make it through this crisis. That's what Jesus tells you when He says come on to me, all of you, and take His yoke and learn of Him, for His yoke is easy and His burden is light.

He promised never to weigh you down with more problems; but, quite the contrary, to ease your load. He's a heavy load bearer.

Become a Cadet (Student in Training) in Christ's Army

Take My **yoke** upon you and **learn of Me**, for I am gentle (meek) and humble (lowly) in heart, and you will find rest (relief and ease and refreshment and recreation and blessed quiet) for your souls.

Matthew 11:29 (Amplified Bible)

A yoke is to join, a coupling, a law, are obligation, pain of balances, the beam of the balance, and serving to couple two things together. He wants you to join yourself together with Him and to learn everything there is to know about Him.

Let me list what Jesus actually did for you. This

will allow you to read for yourself how He came,

lived, and died for you.

Christ Came

For God so greatly loved and dearly prized the world that He [*even*] gave up His only begotten (unique) Son, so that whoever believes in (trusts in, clings to, relies on) Him shall not perish (come to destruction, be lost) but have eternal (everlasting) life. For God did not send the Son into the world in order **to judge (to reject, to condemn, to pass sentence on**) the world, but that the world might find salvation and be made safe and sound through Him. Joh 3:18 He who believes in Him [*who clings to, trusts in, relies on Him*] **is not judged** [*he who trusts in Him never comes up for judgment; for him there is no rejection, no condemnation--he incurs no damnation*]; but **he who does not believe (cleave to, rely on, trust in Him) is judged already** [*he has already been convicted and has already received his sentence*] because he has not believed in and trusted in the name of the only begotten Son of God. [*He is condemned for refusing to let his trust rest in Christ's name.*]

FAITH TO STAY CALM IN A CRISIS

John 3:16-18 (Amplified Bible)

Just as the Father raises up the dead and gives
them life [*makes them live on*], even so the Son
also gives life to whomever He wills and is pleased
to give it. Even the Father judges no one, for He
has given all judgment (the last judgment and the
whole business of judging) entirely into the hands
of the Son, So that all men may give honor
(reverence, homage) to the Son just as they give
honor to the Father. [*In fact*] whoever does not
honor the Son does not honor the Father, Who has
sent Him. I assure you, most solemnly I tell you,
the person whose ears are open to My words [*who
listens to My message*] and believes and trusts in
and clings to and relies on Him Who sent Me has
(possesses now) eternal life. **And he does not
come into judgment** [*does not incur sentence of
judgment, will not come under condemnation*],
but he has already passed over out of death into
life.

John 5:21-24 (Amplified Bible)

FAITH TO STAY CALM IN A CRISIS

Christ Consumed Our Penalty

Christ purchased our freedom [*redeeming us*] from the curse (doom) of the Law [*and its condemnation*] by [*Himself*] becoming a curse for us, for it is written [*in the Scriptures*], Cursed is everyone who hangs on a tree (is crucified); [*Deut. 21:23.*] Gal 3:14 To the end that through [*their receiving*] Christ Jesus, the blessing [*promised*] to Abraham might come upon the Gentiles, so that we through faith might [*all*] receive [*the realization of*] the promise of the [*Holy*] Spirit.

Galatians 3:13-14 (Amplified Bible)

Christ Cancelled the Condemnation

However, I am telling you nothing but the truth when I say it is profitable (good, expedient, advantageous) for you that I go away. Because if I do not go away, the Comforter (Counselor, Helper, Advocate, Intercessor, Strengthener, Standby) will not come to you [*into close fellowship with you*]; but if I go away, I will send Him to you [*to be in close fellowship with you*]. And when He comes, He will convict and convince the world and bring demonstration to it **about sin** and **about righteousness** (uprightness of heart and right standing with God) and about judgment: About sin, because **they do not believe in Me** [*trust in, rely on, and adhere to Me*]; About righteousness (uprightness of heart and right standing with God), because I go to My Father, and you will see Me no longer; About judgment, because the ruler (evil genius, prince) of this world [*Satan*] is judged and condemned and sentence already is passed upon him.

John 16:7-11 (Amplified Bible)

Nor is the free gift at all to be compared to the effect of that one [*man's*] sin. For the sentence [*following the trespass*] of one [*man*] **brought condemnation,** whereas the **free gift [*following*] many transgressions brings justification (an act of righteousness).** For if because of one man's trespass (lapse, offense) death reigned through that one, much more surely will those **who receive [*God's*] overflowing grace (unmerited favor) and the free gift of righteousness [*putting them into right standing with Himself*] reign as kings in life through the one Man Jesus Christ (the Messiah, the Anointed One).** Well then, as one man's trespass [*one man's false step and falling away led*] **to condemnation for all men**, so **one Man's act of righteousness [*leads*] to acquittal and right standing with God and life for all**

men. For just as by one man's disobedience
(failing to hear, heedlessness, and carelessness) the
many were constituted sinners, so by one Man's
obedience the many will be constituted righteous
(made acceptable to God, brought into right
standing with Him).

Romans 5:16-19 (Amplified Bible)

Christ Conquered Sin

He personally **bore our sins in His [*own*] body** on
the tree [*as on an altar and offered Himself on it*],
that we might die (cease to exist) to sin and live to
righteousness. By His wounds you have been
healed. For you were going astray like [*so many*]
sheep, but now you have come back to the
Shepherd and Guardian (the Bishop) of your souls.

I Peter 2:24-25 (Amplified Bible)

MY LITTLE children, I write you these things so
that you may not violate God's law and sin. But if
anyone should sin, **we have an Advocate (One
Who will intercede for us) with the Father--[*it
is*] Jesus Christ** [*the all*] righteous [*upright, just,
Who conforms to the Father's will in every
purpose, thought, and action*]. And He [*that same
Jesus Himself*] is the propitiation (the atoning

sacrifice) for our sins, and not for ours alone but also for [*the sins of*] the whole world.

I John 2:1-2 (Amplified Bible)

It is my desire that all of these scriptures will show you just how much God loves you. That He would send His only son into the world to die for your sins and to provide you with a good life. A life filled with comfort and joy. A life protected by Him. All He asks is that you come to Him, trust your life with Him, and watch Him provide the rest you need for your soul.

Listen to what His word says about His comfort in times of trouble found in the book of Second Corinthians 1: 1-4.

Grace (favor and spiritual blessing) to you and [*heart*] peace from God our Father and the Lord

Jesus Christ (the Messiah, the Anointed One). Blessed be the God and Father of our Lord Jesus Christ, the Father of sympathy (pity and mercy) and the God [*Who is the Source*] of every comfort (consolation and encouragement), Who comforts (consoles and encourages) us in every trouble (calamity and affliction), so that we may also be able to comfort (console and encourage) those who are in any kind of trouble or distress, with the comfort (consolation and encouragement) with which we ourselves are comforted and consoled.

II Corinthians 1:2-4 (Amplified Bible)

His promise is that not only will you receive

comfort from your troubles, but you will get to a

point where you will be able to provide this

comfort to others who find themselves in similar

troubles as you once were. Wow, isn't that great

news that you have such a loving Father who cares

that much about you? That He would heal you to

the degree that you can be used by Him to heal

others. I want you to thank Him now by raising

your hands and opening your mouth and saying

thanks.

Additional Benefits for Coming to Christ: Peace

THEREFORE, SINCE we are justified (acquitted, declared righteous, and given a right standing with God) through faith, let us [*grasp the fact that we*] have [*the peace of reconciliation to hold and to enjoy*] peace with God through our Lord Jesus Christ (the Messiah, the Anointed One). Through Him also we have [*our*] access (entrance, introduction) by faith into this grace (state of God's favor) in which we [*firmly and safely*] stand. And let us rejoice and exult in our hope of experiencing and enjoying the glory of God. Moreover [*let us also be full of joy now!*] let us exult and triumph in our troubles and rejoice in our sufferings, knowing that pressure and affliction and hardship produce patient and unswerving endurance. And endurance (fortitude) develops maturity of character (approved faith and tried integrity). And character [*of this sort*] produces [*the habit of*] joyful and confident hope of eternal salvation.

FAITH TO STAY CALM IN A CRISIS

Romans 5:1-4 (Amplified Bible)

Safety

AND THE Lord said to Noah, Come with all your household into the ark, for I have seen you to be righteous (upright and in right standing) before Me in this generation.

Genesis 7:1 (Amplified Bible)

Fellowship

Dwell in Me, and I will dwell in you. [*Live in Me, and I will live in you.*] Just as no branch can bear fruit of itself without abiding in (being vitally united to) the vine, neither can you bear fruit unless you abide in Me. I am the Vine; you are the branches. Whoever lives in Me and I in him bears much (abundant) fruit. However, apart from Me [*cut off from vital union with Me*] you can do nothing. If a person does not dwell in Me, he is thrown out like a [*broken-off*] branch, and withers; such branches are gathered up and thrown into the fire, and they are burned. If you live in Me [*abide vitally united to Me*] and My words remain in you and continue to live in your hearts, ask whatever you will, and it shall be done for you. When you bear (produce) much fruit, My Father is honored and glorified, and you show and prove yourselves to be true followers of Mine. I have loved you, [*just*] as the Father has loved Me; abide in My love [*continue in His love with Me*].

John 15:4-9 (Amplified Bible)

Eternal Security

The sheep that are My own hear and are listening to My voice; and I know them, and they follow Me. And I give them eternal life, and they shall never lose it or perish throughout the ages. [*To all eternity they shall never by any means be destroyed.*] And no one is able to snatch them out of My hand. My Father, Who has given them to Me, is greater and mightier than all [*else*]; and no one is able to snatch [*them*] out of the Father's hand. I and the Father are One.

John 10:27-30 (Amplified Bible)

The Hundred Fold Lifestyle

Then Peter answered Him, saying, Behold, we have left [*our*] all and have become Your disciples [*sided with Your party and followed You*]. What then shall we receive? Jesus said to them, Truly I say to you, in the new age [*the Messianic rebirth of the world*], when the Son of Man shall sit down on the throne of His glory, you who have [*become My disciples, sided with My party and*] followed Me will also sit on twelve thrones and judge the twelve tribes of Israel. And anyone and everyone who has left houses or brothers or sisters or father or mother or children or lands for My name's sake will receive many [*even a hundred*] times more and will inherit eternal life.

St. Matthews 19:27-29 (Amplified Bible)

HEALTH CONFESSION

Father, I thank you that by the stripes of Jesus I am healed, resisting sickness and disease. I boldly declare that I walk in divine health in my body, my mind, and my emotions in the name of Jesus. I thank you, Father, that because of my covenant and because I honor and worship you, no plague or epidemic comes near or into my house, affecting me or my family. Every harmful germ, virus, or disease that touches my body must die immediately. God, I thank you that you satisfy my lips with those foods that are good and healthy for my body. I will live and not die so I may continue to declare the works of the Lord, in the name of Jesus. Amen!

Please list your prayer needs and testimonies

here:

_____

_____

_____

_____

_____

_____

_____

_____

_____

_____

_____

Chapter Four

Canticle
Continually

Canticle means a song, poem, or hymn of praise. It is to sing songs of praise to God or to write a beautiful poem of your love for Him. I know you're saying how in the world am I going to sing songs of praise in times of crisis? How am I expected to worship when my heart is broken? I don't know how all these problems are going to turn around. I just don't feel like singing or praising God right now. To be honest, I'm wondering did He cause these problems I'm facing right now? How can I worship a God who either caused or allowed these problems I'm facing?

I know your mind is filled with these and perhaps more unanswered questions. I know you are blaming yourself or worse, God, for the problems you're facing.

I want you to take a deep breath and take a journey with me through this chapter and let's see if we can answer these questions, or at least try to make sense of it all.

Let's read what the Bible says about temptation and trouble in the book of James to get a good idea if God uses problems or trouble to cause us grief or worse, to train or teach us lessons.

Let no man say when he is tempted, I am tempted of God: for God cannot be tempted with evil, neither tempteth he any man: But every man is tempted, when he is drawn away of his own lust, and enticed. Then when lust hath conceived, it bringeth forth sin: and sin, when it is finished, bringeth forth death. Do not err, my beloved brethren. Every good gift and every perfect gift is from above, and cometh down from the Father of

lights, with whom is no variableness, neither
shadow of turning.

Jas 1:13-17 (King James Bible)

Notice the Bible says in the book of James 1:13,

don't let any man say when he is tempted, or you

can say tried, that he is tempted of God. God

cannot be tempted with evil, neither tempted He

any man. Did you hear that? God cannot be

tempted with nor will He tempt any man with evil?

So it is clear beloved, trouble, grief, and all of

those things do not and cannot come from God.

God is not a liar. When He says something, He

means it. All of the problems, trials, tribulations,

and the pain that you are experiencing is not God.

It is always easy when things are not going right

and when crisis arises in our lives or when it seems

like we are in a valley experience to look outwardly to find who is to blame. But, I can assure you as the scriptures just pointed out, God cannot tempt you. Whenever you're being tempted, it is to cause you to fail. That's why God is not tempting you. God will test you, but never will He tempt you. Testing comes to show you where you are in the process. Temptation comes to make you fail. There is no good in temptation.

The scriptures go on to say that whenever lust is conceived, it brings forth sin and death. I'm not saying that you are to blame for what is going wrong in your life right now. I'm trying to show you that it's not God who is the cause of these problems. I think it's easy for us to point the finger at Him when things are not going well in our lives, but if we study the scriptures and get a better understanding of who God really is, we will discover that He's not in the temping business.

I really want you to focus on verse 17. It says that every good and perfect gift comes from God. It then stands to reason that He's not the one that causes bad things to happen in our lives.

Let's look at some of the names of God to see if He has a name that means trial, trouble, grief, or pain.

God- who He is to us

- Jehovah/Yahweh- I am who I am
- Jehovah Jireh- the Lord will provide (Ge 22:14)
- Jehovah Nissi- The Lord is my

banner (Ex 17:15)
- Jehovah Shalom- The Lord is peace
  (Judg 6:24)
- Jehovah Shammah- The Lord is there
  (Ezek 48:35)
- Jehovah Tsebaoth- The Lord of host
  (I Sam 1:3)

I want you to notice that every one of these names mean something about His character. He is a good God and worthy of all the praise and worship we could ever give Him.

There are several reasons for crisis and problems to arise in our lives. These can be but are not limited to the following:

A.) **Human Era**- sometimes we make mistakes

B.) **Satanic Attack**- the devil is attacking

C.) **Natural Causes**- Things wear out or just

doesn't work

The point is, God's heart toward you is for your

good only. He is never trying to hurt you. If it was

His desire to hurt you, He would have never sent

His only son to die a gruesome death in order to

save you.

Let's now move to why I believe even in the midst

of this season of trouble that you're going through,

you can still canticle the Lord.

The Purpose Of Praise

I will give to the Lord the thanks due to His
rightness and justice, and I will sing praise to the
name of the Lord Most High.

Psalm 7:17 (Amplified Bible)

The purpose of praise is to tell God how good He is and to lavish upon Him all of the praise you can. It is to understand that He is worth all of the glory and the praise that you can give Him. Praise is to value the object of your praise. When you begin to see and to understand God's worth; it won't be a difficult thing to praise Him.

The Bible says in the book of Psalms 7:17, I will give to the Lord thanks due to His righteousness and justice, and I will sing praise to the name of the Lord Most High.

The psalmist has decided that God is worth praising. As I previously stated, God will never tempt you. He is not the cause of problems; therefore, He is worthy to be praised. No matter where life finds you, no matter what's going on in

your life, I want you to focus on the goodness of

our God. It is only then that you will be able to

praise a God that you see worth in.

Listen to what the Bible says in Psalms 9.

To the Chief Musician; set for [*possibly*] soprano
voices. A Psalm of David. I WILL praise You, O
Lord, with my whole heart; I will show forth
(recount and tell aloud) all Your marvelous works
and wonderful deeds! I will rejoice in You and be
in high spirits; I will sing praise to Your name, O
Most High!

Psalm 9:1 (Amplified Bible)

Notice the psalmist says in verse 2 that he will

rejoice in high spirit. He says this because despite

all of the things going wrong in his life, he realizes

that he would be nothing without God on his side.

He knows that life would be nothing without God.

FAITH TO STAY CALM IN A CRISIS

God is the very breath of his existence. It is to develop a mentality that you are going to praise God no matter what. I'm not asking you to forget about what's going on in your life, nor am I suggesting that it doesn't hurt, but what I am saying is that focusing on who's to blame or trying to find out whose fault it is, will not help. Remember the goodness of God and praise Him in it, not for it.

In everything give thanks: for this is the will of God in Christ Jesus concerning you.

I Thessalonians 5:18 (King James Bible)

The purpose of praise is to see the worth of the object of your praise and to develop a proper perspective about the problems. This crisis is not the end of you. He will not allow it to crush you or destroy you. Find the strength to open your mouth,

lift up your hands and tell a good God that you

love Him, that you honor Him, and that you trust

Him with your heart during the crisis. Let Him

bring a calm into your spirit that will allow you to

bare it.

The Participants Of Praise

Through Him, therefore, let us constantly and at all
times offer up to God a sacrifice of praise, which is
the fruit of lips that thankfully acknowledge and
confess and glorify His name.

Hebrews 13:15 (Amplified Bible)

Notice it says that we will constantly and

continually offer up to God a sacrifice of praise.

Praising God can sometimes be a sacrifice. We

don't always feel like praising God when we're

tired, sad, or upset. That's why it's called a

sacrifice of praise. You can't sit on the sideline of

life hoping that others will do for you what you

need to do for yourself, and praising God is one of

those things you must do for yourself. You must

participate in praising God.

Psalm 150:6 says, Let everything that hath breath

praise the LORD. Praise ye the LORD.

Being an active participant in praising God is good

for your soul and your health because it takes your

mind and thoughts off of the negatives and focus

on the positives. It causes you to think of the

goodness of God and all He's done for you. It

literally makes God big and your problems

smaller. Decide today that you are going to praise

Him no matter what and do it.

The Power Of Praise

[*A Psalm*] of David; when he pretended to be
insane before Abimelech, who drove him out, and
he went away. I WILL bless the Lord at all times;
His praise shall continually be in my mouth. My
life makes its boast in the Lord; let the humble
and afflicted hear and be glad. O magnify the
Lord with me, and let us exalt His name together.
I sought (inquired of) the Lord and required Him
[*of necessity and on the authority of His Word*],
and He heard me, and delivered me from all my
fears. [*Ps. 73:25; Matt. 7:7.*] They looked to Him
and were radiant; their faces shall never blush for
shame or be confused. This poor man cried, and
the Lord heard him, and saved him out of all his
troubles. The Angel of the Lord encamps around
those who fear Him [*who revere and worship Him
with awe*] and each of them He delivers. [*Ps.
18:1; 145:20.*] O taste and see that the Lord [*our
God*] is good! Blessed (happy, fortunate, to be
envied) is the man who trusts and takes refuge in
Him. [*I Pet. 2:2, 3.*] O fear the Lord, you His
saints [*revere and worship Him*]! For there is no

want to those who truly revere and worship Him
with godly fear

Psalms 34:1-9 (Amplified Bible)

Praising God has the power to transform your

thinking and to elevate your thoughts. It will cause

you to see things differently. You will see God in a

better light than you previously viewed Him. You

see, praise is a heart changer. It fills your heart

with gratitude not despair. David realized how

good God had been to him and Israel. He then

asked the people to acknowledge the goodness of

God by tasting and seeing that He is good. David

says for there is no want to those who truly revere

and worship Him with godly fear. Worshiping God

has the power to meet your needs without you

even asking. God knows everything you need, and

He's always ready to meet those needs. He knows the trouble you find yourself in right now. Remember, He's working all things together for your good - that means the good and the bad. Never treat God bad in the middle of a bad situation, before you see the end of the thing. He's causing even the bad to work out for your good. Give Him time to work His plan out, and you will see that He's for you and not against you. In the meanwhile, decide to praise Him right there in the trouble.

The Passion Of Praise

The passion of praise is a heart that realizes that God is good all the time, and all the time God is good. It's a heart filled with gratitude for the thing God has already done in the past.

It's a heart that understands that bad things don't define a good God. It's a heart that is filled with overflowing love and commitment to never stop giving a good God your best praise no matter what happens in life or no matter where life finds you.

I want you to draw on the love you have for God and to express that love through your worship for Him. Let Him know that you're grateful and thankful for everything He's already done in your life and for the things you believe He will do. Open your mouth and lift up your hands to a good, good Father who loves you unconditionally.

Remember it was His passion first given to you through His son's death on a cross that should birth your passion toward Him with a heart of thanksgiving. He gave first, so you give now.

Listen to what the Bible says about the love of God toward you in Romans 5:1-11

Therefore being justified by faith, we have peace with God through our Lord Jesus Christ: By whom also we have access by faith into this grace wherein we stand, and rejoice in hope of the glory of God. And not only *so,* but we glory in tribulations also: knowing that tribulation worketh patience; And patience, experience; and experience, hope: And hope maketh not ashamed; because the love of God is shed abroad in our hearts by the Holy Ghost which is given unto us. For when we were yet without strength, in due time Christ died for the ungodly. For scarcely for a righteous man will one die: yet peradventure for a good man some would even dare to die. But God commendeth his love toward us, in that, while we were yet sinners, Christ died for us. Much more then, being now justified by his blood, we shall be saved from wrath through him. For if, when we were enemies, we were reconciled to God by the death of his Son, much more, being reconciled, we shall be saved by his life. And not only *so,* but we also joy in God through our Lord Jesus Christ, by whom we have now received the atonement.

Romans 5:1-11 (King James Bible)

It is my prayer that having read through this chapter and discovering the love of a good God has caused you to become more intimately acquainted with Him and has caused your heart to be filled with love and the desire to praise Him even more. I pray that your thoughts toward Him are good, and your thoughts concerning the outcome of your crisis is positive. I hope you now know that God is for you and not against you. He is the one who will never leave or forsake you in your time of need. He has a plan for your life that will come to pass no matter what problems or

crisis has arisen. You can now canticle Him continually.

HEALTH CONFESSION

Father, I thank you that by the stripes of Jesus I am healed, resisting sickness and disease. I boldly declare that I walk in divine health in my body, my mind, and my emotions in the name of Jesus. I thank you, Father, that because of my covenant and because I honor and worship you, no plague or epidemic comes near or into my house, affecting me or my family. Every harmful germ, virus, or disease that touches my body must die immediately. God, I thank you that you satisfy my lips with those foods that are good and healthy for my body. I will live and not die so I may continue to declare the works of the Lord, in the name of Jesus. Amen!

Please list your prayer needs and testimonies here:

_____

_____

_____

_____

_____

_____

_____

Chapter Five

Cache In
Christ

Cache means a hiding place or to be concealed. It suggests that it's possible to be hidden or concealed from someone or something. It is in times of crisis that we wish to be hidden from all of the trouble that seems to be mounting up against us. I know you wish there was somewhere you could just go and find rest. Let me take you on a journey through this chapter and reveal a place you can do just that - a place where you can find rest from your troubles and peace in the midst of a storm. A place that is high above the pain and trouble. A place that you can be healed, hidden, and high above the crisis that seems to surround you. Let me first tell you about a high place I've founded.

A High Place

The Lord also will be a refuge and a high tower for the oppressed, a refuge and a stronghold in times of trouble (high cost, destitution, and desperation). And they who know Your name [*who have experience and acquaintance with Your mercy*] will lean on and confidently put their trust in You, for You, Lord, have not forsaken those who seek (inquire of and for) You [*on the authority of God's Word and the right of their necessity*]. [*Ps. 42:1.*] Sing praises to the Lord, Who dwells in Zion! Declare among the peoples His doings! For He Who avenges the blood [*of His people shed unjustly*] remembers them; He does not forget the cry of the afflicted (the poor and the humble).

Psalm 9:9-12 (Amplified Bible)

God is such a good father and protector that He provide places of refuge for His people to go in times of trouble. Notice it says in verse 9 that He is a refuge and a high tower for the oppressed. In the book of Numbers 35:6 He asked that six cities be

reserved as cities of refuge.

And among the cities which ye shall give unto the
Levites *there shall be* six cities for refuge, which
ye shall appoint for the manslayer, that he may flee
thither: and to them ye shall add forty and two
cities. *So* all the cities which ye shall give to the
Levites *shall be* forty and eight cities: them *shall
ye give* with their suburbs. And the cities which ye
shall give *shall be* of the possession of the children
of Israel: from *them that have* many ye shall give
many; but from *them that have* few ye shall give
few: every one shall give of his cities unto the
Levites according to his inheritance which he
inheriteth. And the LORD spake unto Moses,
saying, Speak unto the children of Israel, and say
unto them, When ye be come over Jordan into the
land of Canaan; Then ye shall appoint you cities to
be cities of refuge for you; that the slayer may flee
thither, which killeth any person at unawares. And
they shall be unto you cities for refuge from the
avenger; that the manslayer die not, until he stand
before the congregation in judgment. And of these
cities which ye shall give six cities shall ye have
for refuge. Ye shall give three cities on this side
Jordan, and three cities shall ye give in the land of
Canaan, *which* shall be cities of refuge. These six
cities shall be a refuge, *both* for the children of
Israel, and for the stranger, and for the sojourner

among them: that every one that killeth any person unawares may flee thither.

Numbers 35:6-15 (King James Bible)

Six Levitical cities were set aside to provide

shelter and safety for those guilty of manslaughter.

Of the 48 cities assigned to the Levites, six were

designated as cities of refuge, three on either side

of the Jordan River. Wow! God's grace is so

amazing that He made it possible for the guilty to

have a place to go and find shelter. I want you to

think about that for a moment. If God did this in

the Old Testament, how much better is it for you in

the New Testament, which is considered a better

covenant.

The refuge cities served as a place for those who

accidentally killed someone and could go there as an asylum. By fleeing to one of these cities, the person would live according to Deuteronomy 4:41. Then Moses severed three cities on this side of Jordan toward the sun rising - Deuteronomy 4:42. That the slayer might flee thither, which should kill his neighbour unawares, and hated him not in times past; and that fleeing unto one of these cities he might live: If the manslayer reached a city of refuge before the avenger of blood could slay him, he was given a fair trial and provided asylum until the death of the high priest.

In the New Testament, the cities of refuge apparently became a type or symbolic illustration of the salvation that is found in our Lord and

Savior Jesus Christ.

Listen to what the Bible says in the book of

Hebrews 6:13-20

For when God made promise to Abraham, because he could swear by no greater, he swore by himself, Saying, Surely blessing I will bless thee, and multiplying I will multiply thee. And so, after he had patiently endured, he obtained the promise. For men verily swear by the greater: and an oath for confirmation *is* to them an end of all strife. Wherein God, willing more abundantly to shew unto the heirs of promise the immutability of his counsel, confirmed *it* by an oath: That by two immutable things, in which *it was* impossible for God to lie, we might have a strong consolation, who have fled for refuge to lay hold upon the hope set before us: Which *hope* we have as an anchor of the soul, both sure and steadfast, and which entereth into that within the veil; Whither the forerunner is for us entered, *even* Jesus, made an high priest for ever after the order of Melchisedec.

Hebrews 6:13-20 (King James Bible)

The Apostle Paul explains in the book of Romans 5:9 that much more then, being now justified by His blood, we shall be saved from wrath through Him. Regardless of your sin, you can find refuge in Jesus. What a wonderful thing God has provided for you - a high place of refuge, far from the avenger of blood.

The believer is safe forever in the heavenly city of refuge because of the finished work of the cross provided by our high priest Jesus Christ.

A Hiding Place

To the Chief Musician. [*A Psalm*] of the sons of Korah, set to treble voices. A song. GOD IS our Refuge and Strength [*mighty and impenetrable to temptation*], a very present and well-proved help in trouble. Therefore we will not fear, though the earth should change and though the mountains be

shaken into the midst of the seas, Though its
waters roar and foam, though the mountains
tremble at its swelling and tumult. Selah [*pause,
and calmly think of that*]!

Psalm 46:1-3 (Amplified Bible)

Not only did God provide a high place, a place of

refuge and a place where His people can find calm

and find safety, but He also provided a hiding

place that you can find rest and peace in a time to

just recuperate.

Notice what the Bible says in the book of Psalm

46, God is our refuge and strength, a very present

and well-proven help in trouble. I want you to look

at what it says, He is mighty and impenetrable.

That means we serve a God that is not just a high

place and not just a hiding place, but that He is our

protector. He is impenetrable, unable to be accessed when the enemy comes. You are literally hidden in Christ, and he cannot penetrate Christ. I want you to picture this. Picture three barrels. There is one small barrel, one medium barrel, and a large barrel. Put the small barrel in the medium barrel and then put the medium barrel inside of the large barrel and seal it. In order to get to the small barrel, you must penetrate access to the large barrel, and so it is with our God. If the enemy thinks he can access you, he must first go through God, and I want to tell you beloved, our God is impenetrable. The enemy cannot access you when you are in a high and hidden place, which is in Christ Jesus. That's why the psalmist says that no matter what comes up against you and no matter

what situation you find yourself in, when you are
hidden in Christ, no weapon formed against you
will prosper. Nothing thrown at you will overtake
you. Isn't that great news?

Listen to what the Bible says in the book of Psalm
32:7. Thou *art* my hiding place; thou shalt
preserve me from trouble; thou shalt compass me
about with songs of deliverance.

God promises to deliver you no matter where life
takes you. No matter what trouble you find
yourself in, always remember you are high and
hidden.

I want you to repeat after me, "I am in a high place
in Christ. I am also in a hidden place in Christ;
therefore, I shall not be afraid.

Again, we are reminded in the book of Psalm 119:114, Thou *art* my hiding place and my shield: I hope in thy word.

Finally, let me tell you the third and final thing that is provided for you when you have been cache in Christ. When you are hidden and concealed in Christ, there is available to you a high place, a hidden place, and then finally a healthy place. Yes, that's right. There is a place in Christ where the healing waters flow. All you have to do is trust God's word and believe that you receive all of His promises.

A Healthy Place

HE WHO dwells in the secret place of the Most High shall remain stable and fixed under the shadow of the Almighty [*Whose power no foe can withstand*]. I will say of the Lord, He is my Refuge and my Fortress, my God; on Him I lean and rely, and in Him I [*confidently*] trust! For [*then*] He will deliver you from the snare of the fowler and from the deadly pestilence. [*Then*] He will cover you with His pinions, and under His wings shall you trust and find refuge; His truth and His faithfulness are a shield and a buckler. You shall not be afraid of the terror of the night, nor of the arrow (the evil plots and slanders of the wicked) that flies by day, Nor of the pestilence that stalks in darkness, nor of the destruction and sudden death that surprise and lay waste at noonday. A thousand may fall at your side, and ten thousand at your right hand, but it shall not come near you. Only a spectator shall you be [*yourself inaccessible in the secret place of the Most High*] as you witness the reward of the wicked. Because you have made the Lord your refuge, and the Most High your dwelling place, [*Ps. 91:1, 14.*] There shall no evil befall you, nor any plague or calamity come near your tent. For He will give His angels [*especial*] charge over you to accompany and defend and preserve you in all your ways [*of obedience and service*]. They shall bear you up on their hands, lest you dash your foot against a stone. [*Luke 4:10, 11; Heb. 1:14.*] You shall tread upon the lion and adder; the young lion and the serpent shall you trample underfoot. [*Luke 10:19.*] Because he has set his love upon Me, therefore will I deliver him; I will set him on high, because he knows and understands My name [*has a personal knowledge of My mercy, love, and kindness--trusts and relies on Me, knowing I will never forsake him, no, never*]. He shall call upon Me, and I will answer him; I will be with him in trouble, I will deliver him and honor him. With long life will I satisfy him and show him My salvation.

Psalm 91:1-16 (Amplified Bible)

I want you to notice what the Bible says in Psalm 91:1. It says he who dwells in the secret place of the most high shall remain stable and fixed under the shadow of the Almighty, no foe can withstand. The key word in this verse is dwells. This word literally means to sit down. Yes, that's right, to sit down. That is a posture of rest when you decide to trust God by making Him your hiding place, your high place, and your healthy place. You must determine in your mind to sit down. It is in this position of rest mentally that your body can recuperate from the stress and pain, and all of the toxicity that has built up because of fear, anxiety and worry.

It also means to sit in quiet. That is a peaceful state, and whenever you allow your mentality to rest in such a way, it calms your surroundings and welcomes peace to come in. I would encourage you right now to take a deep breath, to sit down, and to keep quiet for a moment. Just take it all in and just enjoy being in the presence of the Lord. Allow His grace to fall over you like a waterfall rinsing away all of the dirt and filth of this world. Allow His grace to minister to you as you sit in a quiet place trusting that no matter what you're facing right now, God has you. I want you to remember this, whenever you are at work, God is resting; but, whenever you are resting, God is at work.

Let me tell you of the story about a little woman named Ruth who was married to Naomi's son. One day her husband died, and she decided that she would continue to live with Naomi. Wherever Naomi went, Ruth decided to go. You can find the story in the book of Ruth.

Listen to what Naomi instructed Ruth to do after she went and found work to bring home food in the book of Ruth 3:18.

My daughter, until you learn how the matter turns out for the man, sit still and rest because he will not rest until he finishes the matter today. Naomi is telling Ruth, you've done everything you can do naturally, now sit and rest.

In this story Naomi represents the Holy Spirit, Boaz represents Christ, and Ruth represents you. The Holy Spirit is telling you to rest, sit, and be at peace until Christ works out the problem. This is exactly what God is telling you right now; He is telling you to rest. I understand what you're going through. I know where you are. I know what you're facing. I am well acquainted with your situation, but what I want you to do is to sit and be at rest while I work things out.

I also want you to notice that it says in Psalm 91:2 that the Lord says He is your refuge.

Remember I told you in previous chapters that God is our refuge. I want to give you an acronym for the word refuge. Whenever you look at the word refuge, I want you to say this, Receiving Everything From Under God Every day. Every time you see the word refuge, I want you to be reminded that you Receive Everything From Under God Every day.

In verse 3, He says He will deliver you from the snare of the Fowler and from the deadly pestilence. This is a promise from God that it is His desire that you be healed in this healthy place. The Bible tells us in several places that by Jesus's stripes, we are healed. It tells us in Isaiah 53:5 that by His stripes we are healed. It also tells us in I Peter 2:24 that by His stripes, we were healed.

You see, when you trust the finished work of Jesus Christ on the cross and you come to a place not of toiling, not of panic, but a peaceful place where you can simply sit down and rest, you can receive from God instead of worrying about what to give God.

Now this may sound farfetched, but listen. We serve a God who wants to give unto us and not just receive from us. Remember I told you in the previous chapter why it is important that we praise God. I told you about praise, and the power, and the participant, and the purpose, and the passion of praise. This is a place that is so healthy that God promises that we should not be afraid of the terror by night nor of the arrows by day nor of the pestilence that stalks in the dark. 1,000 may fall at your side and 10,000 at your right hand, but the key here is, that it says, it shall not come near you because you are in a high place, you are in a

hidden place; and, yes, you are in a healthy place.

Can I get you to shout hallelujah to the most high

God for the things that He has done?

Finally, listen to what Psalm 91:10 says. There

shall no evil befall you nor any plague or calamity

come near your tent. That is a promise for when

you are in this high place in Christ that the enemy

cannot reach, and when you are in this hidden

place in Christ that the enemy cannot find, and

when you are in this healthy place that no plague

nor calamities shall come near you, God's got you!

These are the promises of your Father given unto

you.

What I want you to do now is to continually read

Psalm 91 and all of the other scriptures that are in

this book and saturate your mind with His promises concerning your protection and your healing. Not just your protection, but the protection of your whole family. I want you to read the health confession that I have made available at the end of most chapters. Read it out loud and receive its promises.

HEALTH CONFESSION

Father, I thank you that by the stripes of Jesus I am healed, resisting sickness and disease. I boldly declare that I walk in divine health in my body, my mind, and my emotions in the name of Jesus. I thank you, Father, that because of my covenant and because I honor and worship you, no plague or epidemic comes near or into my house, affecting me or my family. Every harmful germ, virus, or disease that touches my body must die immediately. God, I thank you that you satisfy my lips with those foods that are good and healthy for my body. I will live and not die so I may continue to declare the works of the Lord, in the name of Jesus. Amen!

Please list your prayer needs and testimonies here:

_____

_____

_____

_____

_____

Chapter Six

**Cast Your
Concerns On
Christ**

FAITH TO STAY CALM IN A CRISIS

Casting the whole of your care [*all your anxieties, all your worries, all your concerns, once and for all*] on Him, for He cares for you affectionately and cares about you watchfully. [*Ps. 55:22.*]

I Peter 5:7 (Amplified Bible)

I want to talk to you about how to rest and to cast all of your concerns on Christ. You literally do what the Bible tells us to do in I Peter 5:7. It says cast all of your cares on the Lord for He cares for you.

This is what I want you to do. Picture this: picture getting a container. I want you to put everything in your mind in that container. This is how we're going to do it. I want you to get a container, and if you don't have a physical container, I want you to picture one in your mind. Get some paper and

write down everything you're dealing with. I want
you to write sickness, home foreclosure, car
repossession, bad doctors' diagnoses, job
downsizing, divorce papers, on and on, etc. I want
you to write that down, and I want you to put it in
that container.

Now I want you to get a chair, and I want you to
place that chair in the center of your room.
Literally, this is what I want you to do. I want you
to do this for me now. You can do it. I'm right
there with you. You can do it. Those are objects
that I want you to get. If you don't have a
container, get a bucket.

If you're angry right now or if you're hurt or if
you're in denial; I want you to write that down on

the piece of paper. Everything that causes you to feel the way you feel, every bad word you've ever heard in this season of your life. I want you to write that down, and I want you to put that in the bucket or the container.

Get a chair and sit it in the center of the room, and I want you to visualize that God is sitting in that chair. Trust me to muster up enough strength and place that chair in the center of the room. Take your bucket or your container filled with everything that's wrong in your life, and I want you to walk over to that chair as you visualize God in that chair. Don't be fearful. God is not going to be angry with you; He's not going to strike you. He's not going to curse you. Listen to me, and I want you to take that bucket or that container, I want you to dump it at the foot of that chair, and I want you to picture that you are literally casting all of your cares at His feet. I want you to walk away from the chair, my beloved.

This is how you cast your cares on Him by simply dumping at His feet. You see, you will literally find rest when you dump out of your mind all of the things that bring you anguish, anxiety, pain, and trouble. Literally, you must dump these issues out of your mind. It may seem difficult, but if you're truly going to find rest and you're truly going to find a place of rest in your mind, you are going to have to dump what was causing you to feel that way. You see, God offers us an opportunity to come to Him and to cast our cares on Him. This is what I want you to do. This is what I'm literally asking you. It is going to sound strange because when I make this statement, and I'm not trying to upset you or make you more angry, but when I make this statement, I want you to take a deep breath and just trust me for a moment.

Repeat this statement: I don't care. Say it again: I don't care. Now, I'm not asking you not to care in the sense that you're not going to do what you need to do.

What I am asking you is not to carry the weight of that care in your mind on a daily basis because you see, you casted your cares on Him.

You must let Him carry the weight of it. You let Him deal with it while you are being led by Him to do what you need to do without the weight of the trouble that's causing you the pain and the grief that you're going through.

Remember, the Bible tells us to cast our cares on Him, for He cares about us. I have repeatedly said God is not mad with you. God is not after you. God is not trying to hurt you. He is not the cause of any of this, and He is not the reason for the cause of your pain. He is not judging you. He is not trying to hurt you, and God is not trying to teach you some lesson by causing you to go through the pain that you're going through.

Listen to me, and I want you to really think about this. If you have children of your own and you love those children, you would do anything for them. There is nothing you would not do or give up for your kids to have advantages in life. True or false? I want you to answer true or false. Then why do you think and why do you allow your mind to even begin to wrap itself around the thought that a loving God would be trying to teach you a lesson by bringing you through pain and anguish in the worst season of your life?

The Bible tells us that if we know how to give our children good gifts, how much more does our Heavenly Father desire to give us good gifts.

I want you to read these Decrees and Declarations out loud and let it saturate your heart and mind.

Psalm 91 Decree & Declarations

- **I DECREE AND DECLARE THAT I WILL DWELL IN THE SHELTER OF THE MOST HIGH GOD!**

- **I DECREE AND DECLARE THAT I WILL FIND REST IN THE SHADOW OF THE ALMIGHTY!**

- **I DECREE AND DECLARE THAT GOD IS MY REFUGE AND MY FORTRESS!**

- **I DECREE AND DECLARE THAT YOU ARE MY GOD, IN WHOM I TRUST AND WITH GREAT CONFIDENCE IN WHOM I WILL RELY!**

- **I DECREE AND DECLARE THAT GOD WILL RESCUE ME FROM EVERY TRAP AND PROTECT ME FROM EVERY DISEASE!**

- **I DECREE AND DECLARE THAT I AM COVERED AND PROTECTED BY HIS OUTSTRECTHED ARMS!**

- **I DECREE AND DECLARE THAT GOD'S FAITHFUL PROMISES ARE MY ARMOR AND PROTECTION!**

- **I DECREE AND DECLARE THAT I WILL NOT BE AFRAID OF THE TERRORS OF THE NIGHT NOR OF THE ARROWS THAT FLY IN THE DAY!**

- **I DECREE AND DECLARE THAT I WILL NOT DREAD ANY DISEASE THAT STALKS IN THE DARKNESS NOR ANY DISEASE THAT STRIKES AT MIDDAY!**

- **I DECREE AND DECLARE THAT BECAUSE GOD IS MY REFUGE AND THE ALMIGHTY GOD OF MY HOME, NO EVIL CAN DEFEAT ME AND NO PLAGUE CAN COME NEAR MY DWELLING!**

- **I DECREE AND I DECLARE THAT GOD HAS ORDERED HIS ANGELS TO GUARD, DEFEND, AND PROTECT ME AND MY HOUSE!**

- **I DECREE AND DECLARE THAT GOD'S ARMIES OF HEAVEN WILL KEEP ME FROM FALLING; I WILL WALK UNHARMED AND KICK ANYTHING THAT IS EVIL FROM MY PATH!**

- **I DECREE AND DECLARE THAT BECAUSE OF GOD'S LOVE FOR ME, I WILL CALL UPON HIM; HE WILL SET ME ABOVE ALL MY TROUBLES; HE WILL DELIVER ME FROM ALL OF MY FEARS, AND HE WILL HONOR ME WITH HIS PRESENCE AND POWER!**

- **I DECREE AND DECLARE THAT HE WILL REWARD ME WITH LONG**

LIFE; I SHALL LIVE AND NOT DIE,

AND HE WILL SHOW ME HIS

SALVATION!

I want you to read this to yourself on a daily basis and to comfort your heart and your mind with the promises God made to you in Psalm 91.

_____

_____

_____

_____

_____

_____

_____

_____

_____

Chapter Seven

Cachet
Contentment

Cachet is a mark of distinction or authenticity. It is to be identified by a distinctive mark and by real authenticity. When someone looks at you and notice your lifestyle, he or she can see that there is something distinctively different about you, you have been bought with a price of the precious blood of Jesus Christ and you have been marked for eternity. God so loved you that He deposited His Spirit into your spirit, keeping you secured until the day of redemption. That Spirit lives within you and distinguishes you from others. You see, all you need to do is to draw on the power of the Holy Spirit, who is already in operation in your life. This is considered the free grace of God, unearned, unmerited, and undeserved. He desires to be the power by which you use to make it through these crises and calamities that you're facing.

I am not asking you to draw on willpower or human strength. I'm reminding you that you have been marked as a child of the most high God, and there is such a power readily available for you right now.

Let's take a look at II Timothy 1:7 and see what it says about this different kind of power that has been deposited in your life.

For God did not give us a spirit of timidity (of cowardice, of craven and cringing and fawning fear), but [*He has given us a spirit*] of power and of love and of calm and well-balanced mind and discipline and self-control.

II Timothy 1:7 (Amplified Bible)

I want you to pay close attention to what verse 7 says. It says God did not give us a spirit of timidity or fawning fear, but rather He has given us a Spirit of power, love, and a sound and well-balanced mind.

Listen to what Proverbs 14:30 says, A calm and undisturbed mind and heart are the life and health of the body, but envy, jealousy, and wrath are like rottenness of the bones.

Authentic Contentment

Contentment is to be satisfied. The Greek meaning is to be sufficient, to be possessed of sufficient strength, to be strong, to be enough for a thing, to defend, ward off. Sufficient means as much that is needed or desired. The Greek definition means to suffice, enough.

Authentic contentment is something that you already possess. All you have to do is draw on the grace of God to activate what already exists. I don't want you believing that you can't handle this crisis or that there is some outward power or some philosophy or some witchcraft, voodoo, or magic that you need to draw from. You have been given authentic contentment from God. Now, let's draw upon this power that may be lying dormant inside of you.

Let's see what the Bible says in the book of Philippians 4:6 to get a better understanding of how you can literally be content in all situations and circumstances. That it is possible that no

matter what crisis you may be facing, all you have

to do is depend on the grace of God to activate the

power to be content.

Do not fret or have any anxiety about anything, but
in every circumstance and in everything, by prayer
and petition (definite requests), with thanksgiving,
continue to make your wants known to God. And
God's peace [*shall be yours, that tranquil state of a
soul assured of its salvation through Christ, and so
fearing nothing from God and being content with
its earthly lot of whatever sort that is, that peace*]
which transcends all understanding shall garrison
and mount guard over your hearts and minds in
Christ Jesus.

Philippians 4:6-7 (Amplified Bible)

Listen to what Paul says in Philippians 4:6. He

says do not fret or have any anxiety about

anything. He is literally telling you that no matter

what life throws at you and no matter where you

find yourself, and no matter what situations may come, do not fret or be full of anxiety.

I can hear your thoughts. You are literally saying to yourself and asking me a question: do you mean to tell me that with all of the troubles that I'm facing and with all of the situations and issues that are mounting in my life, that I have the authority to control my response? Yes, I am. But, hold on a moment. Don't write me off too quickly. Don't slam the book down and walk away. Just give me a moment. You see, we have been made with a free will, and you have been given power by God. He has given to each one of us the power, the resources, and the ability to control our lives.

FAITH TO STAY CALM IN A CRISIS

When Jesus died upon the cross and God raised Him from the dead, He took back the authority that the enemy had- to run roughshod all over our lives.

The enemy can no longer do as he pleases with your life. I am not saying that he won't mess with you, and I am not denying the situations that you're facing, all of which are real. It is a fact that you're facing seemingly unsurmountable issues, but it is not the truth that number one, you are alone, and number two, that you are hopeless.

The reason that I can ask you to be content, satisfied, at peace, and calm in the midst of everything you're going through is because of the authentic contentment power that you have.

It is my desire that you will get to a point where situations will not control your inner peace. That is what I am literally trying to say: the power of the peace that comes with the presence of God in the person of Jesus Christ supersedes outward troubles.

Notice that Paul goes on to say in verse 6, but in every circumstance and in everything by prayer and petition with thanksgiving, continue to make your wants known to God. The key is to listen very closely to what he says. God's peace shall be yours, that tranquil state of a soul assured of its salvation through Christ, and so fearing nothing from God and being content with its earthly lot of whatever sort that is, that peace which transcends all understanding shall garrison and mount and guard over your hearts and minds in Christ Jesus.

Wow! He literally just told you that the contentment that comes from Christ shall guard your heart and your mind because this peace is not a place that you can find, but it is a person in the form of Jesus Christ. Let me repeat that again: peace that guards your heart and minds is not a place, but it is a person and that person is Jesus Christ. I know that we live in a world where people believe in certain kinds of meditation. They would sit perhaps and try to find a place of peace and try to bring their mind and their bodies to a place by breathing right and using breathing techniques and using willpower, trying very hard to find that state of bliss and peacefulness.

I submit to you that it does not matter if there is no noise in a house, nor does it matter if the lighting is just right. The kind of peace that you need that can keep you in your right frame of mind is not in a place but in a person, and that person, again, is Jesus Christ. This is important because you already possess the person of Jesus Christ. If you have accepted Him as your Lord and Savior, all you need to do is to allow Him to rise up in your heart and mind and to calm you down. He stands readily available for you to give Him the permission to take over.

FAITH TO STAY CALM IN A CRISIS

I want you to say this after me: Jesus, I give you the Lordship over my mind and over my heart. I no longer sit on the throne of my own heart and mind, but I relinquish that into your hands. Jesus, I thank you for governing my life and being the Lord and Savior of my life. I thank you, Jesus, that from this day forward, trouble, calamity, anxiety, and fear will no longer live here. You are the peace in my life.

Now, I want you to close your eyes and take a deep breath and just begin to meditate and practice the presence of Jesus Christ in your life. The authenticity of contentment is not something that is provoked or empowered by willpower, but it is activated by the grace of God in allowing the power of the Holy Spirit that is already within you to do what He comes to do, and that is to help you, let Him help. That's what makes contentment the person and the power of a real Holy Spirit working in and through you, and for you.

Anointed Contentment

She girds herself with strength [*spiritual, mental, and physical fitness for her God-given task*] and makes her arms strong and firm. She tastes and sees that her gain from work [*with and for God*] is good; her lamp goes not out, but it burns on continually through the night [*of trouble, privation, or sorrow, warning away fear, doubt, and distrust*].

Proverbs 31:17-18 (Amplified Bible)

Let's look at anointed contentment. When I say anointed contentment, what am I talking about? Let me explain.

We just read previously in this chapter that you have been endowed with the power of the Holy Spirit. It is that Holy Spirit who is the anointing, the power source. Just as previously explained, He stands readily available to assist you in your life. You don't have to search for powers outside of yourself. God has graced you with His very presence in the form of the Holy Spirit.

Let me show you what the Bible says in the scriptures.

We have listed Proverbs 31:17. Listen to this virtuous woman's description. It says she guards herself with strength, spiritual, mental, and physical fitness for her God-given task. Did you hear that she literally takes the initiative to gird herself with strength, (spiritually, mentally, and physically fitness for her God-given task) and makes her arms strong and firm? She knows that if she's going to be able to confront, face, or deal with whatever the day throws at her, that she must prepare herself. That preparation involves not crying or calling someone to do something for her, but her family can trust that she knows how to handle all of life's issues and that she is well equipped to navigate through life's situations by simply making sure that she pulls on and draws from the help that she has. I want you to notice that this is not external help. This is internal help.

Remember this is a portrait of a virtuous woman in Proverbs 31. It uses the words spiritual, mental, and physical fitness.

I am literally telling you in this new covenant that you have because of Jesus's finished work on the cross, you have a better covenant that you can access.

Listen to what it says in verse 18. She tastes and sees that her gain from work with and for God is good. Her lamp goes not out, but it burns on continually through the night of trouble, privation, or sorrow, warning away fear, doubt, and distrust. The key here is that she became a partner with God. Sometimes we sit idly by on the sidelines of our lives hoping and wishing that God would just do something to get us out of these troubles. I submit to you that you are a partner with God because He will never do for you what you can do for yourself, but He will always be ready to assist you.

Listen to what the Bible says in the book of Hebrews 4: 14. It says in as much then as we have a great high priest who has already ascended and passed through the heavens, Jesus, the son of God, let us hold fast our confession of faith in Him. That's the key. Your faith must be in Jesus because He is the author and finisher of your faith. Your faith should start and finish in Him.

He goes on to say in verse 15, for we do not have a high priest who is unable to understand and sympathize and have a shared feeling with our weaknesses and infirmities and liability to the assaults of temptation, but One who has been tempted in every respect as we are, yet without sin.

We serve a savior who is sinless: that makes the difference.

I am not trying to get you to do some laborious toiling in order to be anointed or to fix the problem yourself; I am pointing you to the one who is anointed. Because of His anointing, you have been set apart as His child to receive all that He is.

It goes on to say in verse 16, let us then fearlessly and confidently and boldly draw near to the throne of grace, the throne of God's unmerited favor to us sinners, that we may receive mercy for our failures and find grace to help in good times. For every need appropriated help and well timed help. Did you hear that? Jesus is literally waiting for you to come running like a little child to His throne where He stands readily available to help you?

Let me caution you - this throne, although it is in Heaven, and God is in Heaven, but He has already come down, died on the cross, and now He lives on the inside of your spirit. So when it says to come boldly to the throne of God, it is not telling you to seek outwardly for some distant place but to imagine in your mind that you are going to a place, that is within you to ask the anointed Holy Spirit to help you in a time of need, because Jesus is well acquainted with any and everything life will ever throw at you. What a comfort to know that Jesus came and lived in a human body just so He can know what it would be like. What love and what care!

I want you to repeat after me again and say, "Jesus, I thank you for dying for my sins. I thank You for sending the Holy Spirit to live within my heart. I now ask, Holy Spirit, let me draw upon Your anointing to assist me with all of the crises that I'm facing." I thank You! Now thank the Holy Spirit for helping in Jesus's name Amen.

Available Contentment

Not that I am implying that I was in any personal want, for I have learned how to be content (satisfied to the point where I am not disturbed or disquieted) in whatever state I am. I know how to be abased and live humbly in straitened circumstances, and I know also how to enjoy plenty and live in abundance. I have learned in any and all circumstances the secret of facing every situation, whether well-fed or going hungry, having a sufficiency and enough to spare or going without and being in want. I have strength for all things in Christ Who empowers me [*I am ready for anything and equal to anything through Him Who infuses inner strength into me; I am self-sufficient in Christ's sufficiency*].

Philippians 4:11-13 (Amplified Bible)

Let's talk about the availability of contentment that is ready and available for you to draw from. Notice as we go back to the book of Philippians 4:11 Paul says, not that I am implying that I was in any personal want, for I have learned how to be content. He says he learned how to be content, and that's exactly what you're doing right now.

FAITH TO STAY CALM IN A CRISIS

You are learning how to be content. Not in the absence of trouble, but in the midst of what you're going through.

Your spirit became quiet without even removing the outward problems. I'm not saying that He's not going to assist you in settling the noises on the outside, but what I'm trying to get you to see is that God is so powerful and His contentment is so potent, that it does not depend on the situations to calm down before He brings peace.

Paul I have learned how to be content and satisfied to the point where I am not disturbed or disquieted in whatever state I am. Listen to what He is saying. No matter where life finds him, no matter what situation is popping up, says no matter what state he is in, he learned how to be content. He says I know how to be abased and live humbly in straitened circumstances, and I know also how to enjoy plenty and live in abundance. I have learned in any and all circumstances the secret of facing every situation, whether well fed or going hungry, having a sufficiency and enough to spare, or going without and being in want, to be content.

Listen to what he says in verse 13. He says I have strength for all things in Christ who empowers me. I am ready for anything and equal to anything through Him who infuses inner strength within me, I am self-sufficient in Christ's sufficiency. Wow, that is exactly what I am trying to convey to you at this moment.

Again, I am not minimizing or belittling the circumstances that you're facing.

Certainly it is a fact that we are living in a day of COVID 19. Jobs are closed, schools are closed, businesses are closed, and we have been given a stay-at-home order by the governor. The state and local officials have no insight into these and other situations or real issues, but in the midst of all of this, there is a sufficient power that you, too, can say I am sufficient in Christ's sufficiency. You see, the sufficiency comes through Christ because of what He's already done for you. Believe it or not, He wants to serve and help you right now in this very hour.

I know you probably thought that He was absent. He didn't care. You might even ask God where are You, can You see what I'm facing? Do You even care?

I come to tell you, yes, He does. He cares for you deeply and passionately. You are deeply loved and highly favored. You are the apple of His eye. You are fearfully and wonderfully made, and He's right there with you.

Repeat after me: "Father, I come to Your throne as Your little child thanking You for giving me all of the contentment and the power to enjoy that I need. I thank You for Your darling son, Jesus, who makes all of this available to me." I believe I received His sufficiency and because of Him, I can face whatever life throws at me. I thank You in the name of Jesus Christ, Amen.

Isn't that great news? Isn't it wonderful to know that you are not alone even though you may not be where you want to be? Things may not be going the way you desire, but there is a promise from a God that loves you, that He has never left you, He has never forsaken you, and that He is right here with you helping you to manage all of the crisis life can possibly throw at you.

I want you to take a deep breath and release the stress, the worry, the anxieties, and the concerns about these crises, and when you inhale, I want you to receive the contentment that has been made readily available. Let Him carry you. Let Him love on you. Let Him help you, for you are loved and

you are not alone.

Psalm 91 Decree & Declarations

- **I DECREE AND DECLARE THAT I WILL DWELL IN THE SHELTER OF THE MOST HIGH GOD!**

- **I DECREE AND DECLARE THAT I WILL FIND REST IN THE SHADOW OF THE ALMIGHTY!**

- **I DECREE AND DECLARE THAT GOD IS MY REFUGE AND MY FORTRESS!**

- **I DECREE AND DECLARE THAT YOU ARE MY GOD, IN WHOM I TRUST AND WITH GREAT CONFIDENCE IN WHOM I WILL RELY!**

- **I DECREE AND DECLARE THAT GOD WILL RESCUE ME FROM EVERY TRAP AND PROTECT ME FROM EVERY DISEASE!**

- **I DECREE AND DECLARE THAT I AM COVERED AND PROTECTED BY HIS OUTSTRECTHED ARMS!**

- **I DECREE AND DECLARE THAT GOD'S FAITHFUL PROMISES ARE MY ARMOR AND PROTECTION!**

- **I DECREE AND DECLARE THAT I WILL NOT BE AFRAID OF THE TERRORS OF THE NIGHT NOR OF THE ARROWS THAT FLY IN THE DAY!**

- **I DECREE AND DECLARE THAT I WILL NOT DREAD ANY DISEASE THAT STALKS IN THE DARKNESS NOR ANY DISEASE THAT STRIKES AT MIDDAY!**

- **I DECREE AND DECLARE THAT BECAUSE GOD IS MY REFUGE AND THE ALMIGHTY GOD OF MY HOME, NO EVIL CAN DEFEAT ME, AND NO PLAGUE CAN COME NEAR MY DWELLING!**

- **I DECREE AND DECLARE THAT GOD HAS ORDERED HIS ANGELS TO GUARD, DEFEND, AND PROTECT ME AND MY HOUSE!**

- **I DECREE AND DECLARE THAT GOD'S ARMIES OF HEAVEN WILL KEEP ME FROM FALLING; I WILL WALK UNHARMED AND KICK ANYTHING THAT IS EVIL FROM MY PATH!**

- **I DECREE AND DECLARE THAT BECAUSE OF GOD'S LOVE FOR ME, I WILL CALL UPON HIM; HE WILL SET ME ABOVE ALL MY TROUBLES; HE WILL DELIVER ME FROM ALL OF MY FEARS, AND HE WILL HONOR ME WITH HIS PRESENCE AND POWER!**

- **I DECREE AND DECLARE THAT HE WILL REWARD ME WITH LONG**

LIFE; I SHALL LIVE AND NOT DIE,

AND HE WILL SHOW ME HIS

SALVATION!

Conclusion

It is my prayer and my desire that this book has been a source of healing for you, and as you peruse through the pages of this book, you have found the strength and the peace that is needed to navigate through life's situations and that the words on the pages of this book have been more than just words.

I hope it have leaped from the pages and become one with you and hidden down in your heart. I hope the words of this book have become a coach and a mentor for you.

I wrote this book because in our present day, COVID 19, the coronavirus, has swept this country and nation like wildfire, and I see people panicking, fearful, worried, and full of anxiety. I have seen some people hopeless about what tomorrow holds, but I pray, again, that this book has settled and calmed all of that and has pointed you to the One who loves you deeply; and, that is Jesus Christ.

I hope you know now that you are not alone; I really hope that you have come to discover that He is right here with you, and for those who already know that, it is my desire that this book served as a coach to simply remind you of the things you may have forgotten or to settle you when days of uncertainties seems to be mounting up against you. I don't know how long you've been quarantined and not allowed to go out, or maybe you have been diagnosed with this COVID 19, but I want you to know that there is hope, and there is a brighter

future ahead for you. This is not the end. Life is

not over. Don't you throw that towel in; don't you

wave that flag. Do not surrender. Your best days

are ahead of you, and there is still a bright future

for you. I am not talking about years from now. I'm

talking about right now, even in the midst of all of

these uncertainties, even in the midst of this

COVID 19 or some sickness or disease, or

calamities that have hit your life. There is a peace

and hope that is made readily available for you;

and, again, it is my desire that as you went through

the chapters of this book, you have discovered all

of the things that if applied can help settle you. It

can help calm you. It pointed you to a source of

strength and power that you are not just existing

anymore but that you are ready to thrive and to live your best life.

Beloved, be blessed and know that I'm praying for you even if I don't know you, and I may not even know your name; but, I'm praying for you. You are not alone.

If this book has been a blessing to you, please consider emailing me at kwa@kwa.life, and share your testimony.

To find more materials like this, please visit us at www.kwa.life.

www.ingramcontent.com/pod-product-compliance
Lightning Source LLC
Chambersburg PA
CBHW031622040426
42452CB00007B/636